C000181339

What a Day!

by

Mike Anderson

and

Paul Heesome

What a Day!

The Stations of the Cross
for young people

by

Mike Anderson

and

Paul Heesome

First published in 1998 by
KEVIN MAYHEW LTD
Buxhall
Stowmarket
Suffolk IP14 3DJ

© 1998 Mike Anderson and Paul Heesome

The right of Mike Anderson and Paul Heesome to be identified as the
authors of this work has been asserted by them in accordance
with the Copyright, Designs and Patents Act 1988.

The artwork for the stations may be photocopied without
copyright infringement, provided it is used for the purpose for
which it is intended. Reproduction of any of the contents of
this book for commercial purposes is subject to the
usual copyright restrictions.

No other part of this publication may be reproduced,
stored in a retrieval system, or transmitted, in any form
or by any means, electronic, mechanical, photocopying,
recording or otherwise, without the prior written
permission of the publisher.

0 1 2 3 4 5 6 7 8 9

ISBN 1 84003 268 5
Catalogue No 1500232

Cover designed by Jonathan Stroulger
Illustrated by Paul Heesome and pupils of
St. Cuthbert's R.C. High School, St. Helens, Merseyside
Typesetting by Jonathan Stroulger
Printed and bound in Great Britain

CONTENTS

ACKNOWLEDGEMENTS

This Lent resource pack was produced as a collaborative effort by the R.E. and Art Departments of St. Cuthbert's R.C. High School, Berrys Lane, Sutton, St. Helens, Merseyside.

Special thanks go to pupils in Years 8 and 10 who assisted in reviewing first drafts; pupils in Year 9 who helped in devising the artwork; and our colleagues who actually used the materials with their Form groups.

Specific mention must go to the following pupils who were instrumental in producing the artwork for the Stations:

Station 1	Laure Parr
Station 2	Michelle Fairhurst
Station 3	Susie O'Keefe
Station 4	Daniel Pilling
Station 5	Rebecca Jones
Station 6	Craig Finney
Station 7	David Lyon
Station 8	Claire Hockenhull
Station 9	Katie Davock
Station 10	Lucy Brunt
Station 11	Heather Rowson
Station 12	Mark Cooper
Station 13	Rachel Bolton
Station 14	Zoe Boyes
Station 15	Lisa Birchall

To all the above our heartfelt thanks,

Mike Anderson
Paul Heesome

FOREWORD

This is a resource book for Lent, comprising 15 Stations of the Cross and 15 corresponding passages. The idea is to build in each classroom – or church or home – a visual representation of a journey by adding a poster of each station to the wall each day.

Each poster represents one of the Stations of the Cross. With each poster there is a passage. The passage is a monologue in which someone comes home to describe the event he/she has witnessed that day. Some of these people are mentioned in the gospels – others are fictitious. The aim with each, though, is to explore the Station at a personal level.

The monologue can be read aloud in a group worship situation, although it would be best if confident readers were chosen. It would also be advisable for readers to have had a chance to read through the passage beforehand to discern the overall feel and tone of the monologue.

The monologues may in some cases lead on to discussion. For example:

- Station 5 leads readily into a discussion on racism
- Station 8 could provoke discussion on the Holocaust

The materials can be used as leaders see fit, but the mixture of the visual and audio stimuli is to be encouraged. In our school, during registration, each Form group put up one poster of the Stations a day on the wall in their classroom every morning for three weeks. This meant that wherever pupils and staff went there was a reminder of the journey of Jesus. Alternatively the monologues could be combined to become a one-off service of the Stations of the Cross.

The artwork for the Stations may be photocopied without copyright infringement so long as it is used for non-commercial purposes. Why not involve your own art department in re-creating the Stations?

SUGGESTED FORMAT for the DAILY STATION

Introduction

Leader   Today we are reflecting on Station ___ – _____.

Leader   We adore you, O Christ, and we praise you.

All   Because by your holy cross you have redeemed the world.

Leader   And today, we are going to hear . . . 's story.

Monologue

Hello! I'm home! What a day!

Quiet time

A short time of quiet reflection or follow-up questions and answers or special intentions.

Prayer

Leader: Now let's pray:

All: Jesus, you have shown that good always overcomes evil,
that light always overcomes darkness,
that hope always overcomes despair
Because of you, we know that death is not the end
and we thank you. AMEN.

or

All   I love you, Jesus – my love above all things.
I repent with my whole heart for having offended you.
Never permit me to separate myself from you again.
Grant that I may love you always.
Then do with me what you will. AMEN

or

use the prayer at the end of the day's monologue,

or

spontaneous prayer by leader or other,

or

prayer led by pupils who have prepared it for the daily Station.

STATION 1 – JESUS IS CONDEMNED TO DEATH

PILATE

THE GOVERNOR'S STORY

Hello! I'm home! What a day!

There I was in the court, and they brought him to me. Usually the prisoners make excuses and protest their innocence. They say they've been framed – they plead for their lives – you know how it is! And when they're sentenced they usually swear like troopers.

Not this one. He just stood there. The rabble obviously wanted his blood. They were chanting, and it looked for a while as if things could get out of hand. Anyway, they said he was a terrorist. He didn't look like one.

So I asked him. He said I should decide for myself. The cheek of it! Well, I showed him and I satisfied the crowds – I'll bet my popularity ratings have gone through the roof today. You see, you can't be soft with terrorists. So, I organised a bit of torture and then they led him off for public execution.

Strange though, he seemed a decent man – never mind, sometimes you have to make decisions in the interest of public safety. Anyway, I dare say tomorrow everyone will have forgotten his name. Now then – what was his name?

PRAYER

Leader   Lord Jesus,
you were condemned by a man
who gave in to the shouts of the crowd.

Help us to be just and courageous
and not to make decisions
just because they will make us popular.

All   Lord of the Cross,
hear our prayer.

STATION 2 – JESUS TAKES UP HIS CROSS

SAMUEL

THE CARPENTER'S STORY

Hello! I'm home! What a day!

All these executions are keeping me and the lads busy. These blooming Romans seem to want crosses for the crucifixions as and when it suits them. Don't they realise the work that goes into each of them? Me and the lads have to go to the forest and chop down the trees, and in this weather we're sweating cobs. Then we have to strip the bark and shape them. My hands are full of splinters.

Anyway, there was this fellow today who was a bit different. Usually they cry and shout about being innocent, but this one didn't. It was like he had nothing left to say – like he was completely spent. I can't even say he looked angry, just sort of disappointed.

He looked a right mess. They'd already whipped him and then we had to give him the cross. They're not half sadistic those Romans – getting these poor blighters to carry their own cross.

Anything to prolong the agony.

Anyway, when I put the cross on this fellow's back, he groaned and looked at me. Usually, their eyes are full of hate, but this one – he was different – oh! he was hurting all right, but I looked in his eyes and . . . I don't know what it was, but he was different.

I asked the soldiers what his name was, and they told me – but I'm damned if I can remember it.

PRAYER

Leader   Lord Jesus,
you were given a cross to carry
that you did not deserve.

Help us not to place burdens on others
by our demands,
by our expectations
and by our selfishness.

All   Lord of the Cross
hear our prayer.

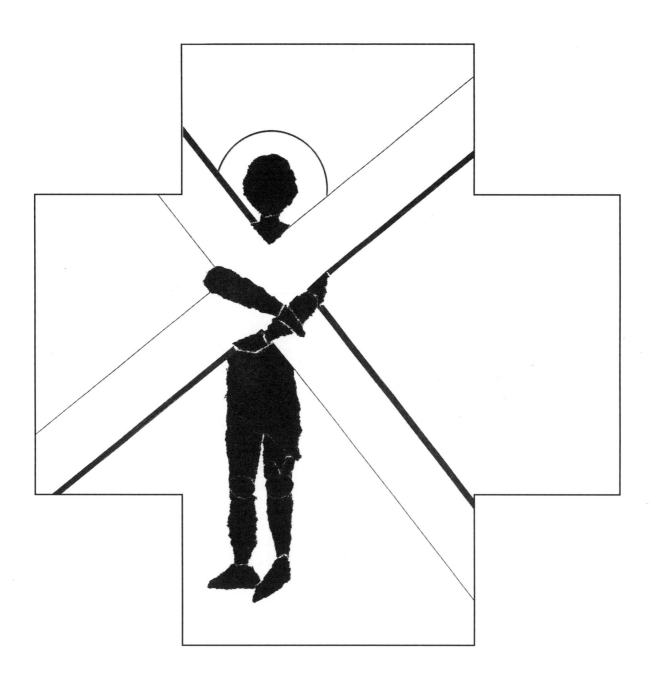

STATION 3 – JESUS FALLS FOR THE FIRST TIME

RACHEL

THE HOUSEWIFE'S STORY

Hello! I'm home! What a day!

I'm getting sick of these executions. There were three more today. How long can it go on for?

Anyway, I was coming back from the market – and I tell you, the price of bread has gone up again – some days I wonder if we're ever going to do more than make ends meet.

Well, me and Miriam were coming through the back streets (the usual short cut) when we got to the main road – and could we get across it? There were loads of people. They just seem to love seeing the criminals suffer. I know they've done wrong, but you know they could just as well chop their heads off – it'd be clean and quick. That's what Roman criminals get – but not our Jewish lads. No – they've got to suffer!

Anyway, there were three today and one was in a really bad way. He'd just fallen when we got to the crossroads, and the soldiers were spitting on him and laughing at him. But, do you know what – he never said a word. He just looked up at them and tried to carry on. I shouted that God would have mercy on him and he looked at me. He managed to pick me out in the crowd somehow. And his eyes just burned into mine, and he opened his lips. I didn't hear what he said – but it looked like he said, 'I know!'

I asked the soldiers who he was and they told me his name. They said it was Yeshua – just like our little boy. 'Yeshua' – 'God saves' – not very appropriate really. I wonder what he'd done.

PRAYER

Leader   Lord Jesus,
you fell under the weight of your cross
but struggled on.

Help us to carry on
when our crosses seem too heavy to bear.

All   Lord of the Cross
hear our prayer.

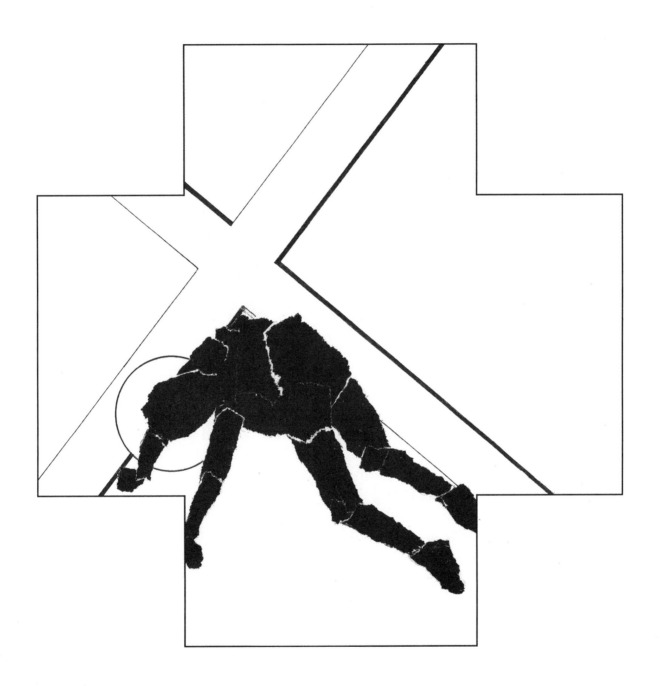

STATION 4 – JESUS MEETS HIS MOTHER

REBEKAH

THE SERVANT GIRL'S STORY

Hello! I'm home! What a day!

Sorry I'm late, Mum, but there was another set of crucifixions, and it was awful.

Do you know who it was? It was that Yeshua, who's been talking about loving enemies and turning the other cheek when someone hits you. You know the one – we heard him when we were visiting Aunt Elizabeth in Galilee. Remember, we went to listen to him – and his friends were pushing us away – but he said, 'Let the children come to me', and he put his arms round each of us and prayed for us.

Remember, he said you had to be like children to enter the Kingdom of Heaven – and everyone said that he'd healed all sorts of people.

It was him all right – bloodstained and exhausted – and just as he came past me a woman ran out into the road and hugged him. It was his mum. You should have seen her – she wept and wept and she was shaking. It was like

someone had put a sword through her heart – like she could feel all his pain.

And he looked at her – and he tried to smile through his own tears. And seeing her just seemed to increase his pain – like he couldn't bear his mum to suffer like that.

And then the soldiers brushed her aside and he went on his way. When they'd moved on, the mother wailed and wailed – an awful sound, I'll never forget it. It was enough to wake the dead.

PRAYER

Leader Lord Jesus,
you met your mother in your suffering.

Help us to appreciate those who care for us
and share with them our joys as well as sorrows.

All Lord of the Cross,
hear our prayer.

STATION 5 – SIMON OF CYRENE CARRIES THE CROSS

SIMON OF CYRENE
THE BLACK MAN'S STORY

Hello! I'm home! What a day!

You'll never guess what happened to me. I was going through town after I'd met with Jacob – that cloth merchant – and I got caught up in a mob that was watching a crucifixion procession. There were three of them and one looked in a particularly bad way – like he'd never get to Golgotha.

As they came past me, the soldiers grabbed me and told me to help him carry the cross.

That's the trouble with being black round here – they automatically think you're fit and strong. And the Romans don't half like reminding you that they're in charge! The racist pigs. Here am I, a visitor to the city, and I get picked out – and of course the Jews loved it, thought it was a great joke.

Anyway – I got hold of the cross and looked at the man. He looked up at me through bloodshot eyes and said,

'Who are you?' I said, 'Simon', and he said with a sigh, 'I've a friend called Simon'.

There was something in his voice that made me calm and made me want to help him. I got filthy as you can see – the cross was already covered with his blood and I got it all over my clothes. But you know, although it seemed humiliating, somehow it also felt like a privilege – like I was doing something worthwhile.

I won't forget what happened today – but I wish I'd asked his name.

PRAYER

Leader   Lord Jesus
you were helped by an outsider
in your society.

Help us to reach out
to those in our lives
who are sometimes outsiders.

All   Lord of the Cross
hear our prayer.

STATION 6 – VERONICA WIPES THE FACE OF JESUS

VERONICA
THE WOMAN'S STORY

Hello! I'm home! What a day!

I got caught up in one of those cruci-fixion parades, and I've been chasing myself all day trying to catch up.

They had this poor bloke – they'd even whipped him earlier on and he was covered in blood and couldn't see where he was going. They'd got some foreigner to help him carry his cross, but he looked like he was going to peg out there and then.

So, I pushed into the street and wiped his face for him and he looked at me – and you know, there was something spooky about the way he did it.

He didn't say anything, but his eyes said 'Thank you' and there was something else in his eyes – a look like I'd done something really special.

I don't know what he'd done – he probably deserved to die – but no one deserves that sort of torture. They'd even put some thorns like a crown on his head and banged them in so that they punctured the skin. Poor so-and-so.

Anyway, I'd best be getting on with the washing – he made a right mess of my towel. Where is it now? Oh, here it is . . . Oh my God! . . . Samuel . . . you'd better come and have a look at this!

PRAYER

Leader   Lord Jesus,
you showed yourself in a special way
to Veronica.

Help us to recognise you
in each other.

All   Lord of the Cross
hear our prayer.

STATION 7 – JESUS FALLS A SECOND TIME

MARCUS

THE SOLDIER'S STORY

Hello! I'm home! What a day!

Another three crucifixions – that Pilate is ruthless. Cross him in any way and that's it – you're for it. We had a couple of petty thieves today and a bloke they said was a terrorist. Well, he deserved it. These Zealot terrorists have killed too many Roman soldiers. It's not safe to walk the streets at night alone.

Mind you – if he was a terrorist, they certainly made an example of him. Should deter some of the others. If you ask me, these Jewish Zealots are off their heads. Freedom for Israel they want. Who are they trying to kid? The Roman Empire will last for ever and will never kowtow to terrorists.

This bloke today though – he's ruined one of my sandals. There he was, carrying the cross – we'd even got this black fellow to help him after he'd fallen over earlier. Well, he falls over again, face first in the dust. The centurion told me to go and get him up. (I felt like telling him to do it himself – then thought better of it.)

So I went over and grabbed him under the arms and heaved him up. That's when I noticed he'd been dripping blood all over my sandal. Made a right mess. So I smacked him one with the shaft of my spear across his face – that soon woke him up. And you'll never guess what happened next – he turned the other side of his face to me and looked at me. It was like he wanted me to hit him there, too.

Like I said – they're off their heads, these Jews.

PRAYER

Leader   Lord Jesus,
you turned your cheek when beaten.

Help us not to retaliate
when we are provoked.

All   Lord of the Cross
hear our prayer.

STATION 8 – JESUS MEETS THE WOMEN OF JERUSALEM

MARTHA
THE FRIEND'S STORY

Hello! I'm home! What a day!

They've done it! I knew he'd go too far, making enemies of the priests and the Pharisees and then the Romans. Poor man – Pilate tried to release him, but the crowd just shouted for his blood – and asked for the release of that thug, Barabbas, instead!

Ruth and I ran back to tell the others and all of us went to see him on his way to Golgotha. It was awful! He stopped when he recognised us and said not to weep for him, but for our children, because one day they were going to suffer. His voice trembled as he said it – like one day all of us Jews were going to be wiped out.

I wonder what he meant. No one in their right mind would try to get rid of an entire people. Even the Romans let us get on with our own business, although they take taxes from us. I can't imagine what he meant, but there was no doubt in his voice – he meant it all right. 'Don't cry for me – cry for your children.'

Oh God, don't let the children suffer! I'm frightened, David, I'm frightened!

PRAYER

Leader Lord Jesus,
the world has suffered many atrocities.
People have been killed for their religion,
their race and their colour.

Help us to make the world a better place
for ourselves and for our children in the future.

All Lord of the Cross
hear our prayer

STATION 9 – JESUS FALLS FOR A THIRD TIME

ISAAC

THE DELIVERY BOY'S STORY

Hello! I'm home! What a day!

It's been murder trying to make my deliveries today. There's so many people about. It's bad enough that it's Passover time with all the country yokels coming to the city, but then I got trapped by the crucifixion parade.

I'm shattered. I had a real rush to get all the deliveries done before sunset. And as for the crucifixions, I've got to say I'm getting fed up of them. They used to be quite a spectacle, but there's just too many now.

Today there were three. One of them was oh so slow. Mind you, they'd already whipped him and he had thorns in his head for some reason. But, talk about slow – he didn't half hold me up.

Anyway, I shouted at the soldiers to get a move on and they kicked him and he fell over. For a moment I thought he'd pegged out there and then, but he stirred and looked up and for a split second his eyes caught mine. It was a weird feeling.

You'd have expected there to be hate, but no, his eyes were full of love – like he cared about me – like I was the one who was suffering. Strange – I wonder what he'd done.

PRAYER

Leader   Lord Jesus,
you suffered indignity upon indignity.

Help us to realise
that we too can overcome
when all seems lost.

All   Lord of the Cross
Hear our prayer.

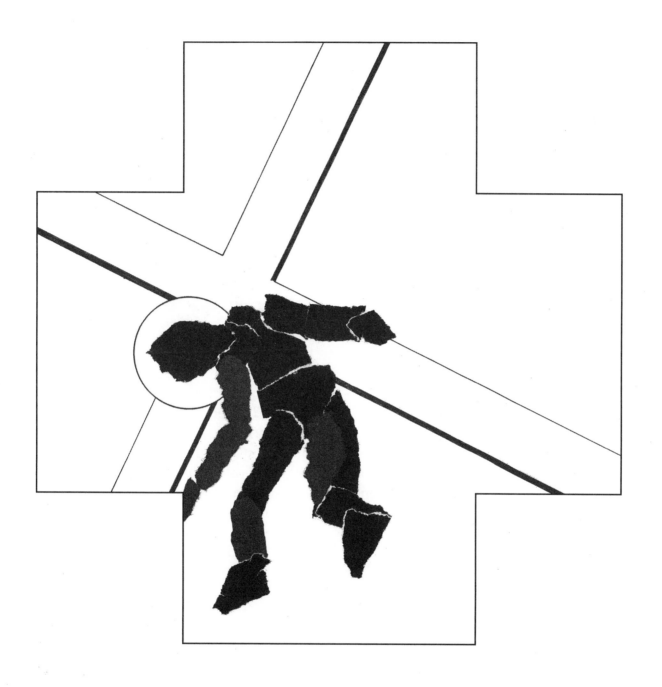

STATION 10 – JESUS IS STRIPPED

JOSEPHINE
THE YOUNG WOMAN'S STORY

Hello! I'm home! What a day!

Sorry I'm late. Don't be angry with me, Dad. I was really busy at Nan's this morning. I did all the cleaning and she was looking a bit better today. She still looks tired though. After I'd done the cleaning, I took the washing and was making my way down to the river when I got held up by a crucifixion parade. Anyway, I don't know why, but I followed it all the way to Golgotha. That place really gives me the creeps – no wonder they call it 'Place of the Skull'. I'd never seen a crucifixion before and I didn't realise how awful it was going to be.

They took the crosses off the criminals – there were three – and then the soldiers stripped their clothes off them. One of them had been whipped earlier and the clothes had stuck to his blood. When the soldiers ripped his clothes off it opened all the wounds and they started bleeding again. They'd even put thorns on his head – like a crown.

And they kept skitting him, saying 'Hail, King of the Jews' in dead sarcastic voices. And there he was – naked. They weren't just stripping him of his clothes – it was like they were stripping him of his dignity, too.

But, Dad, there was something about him. He never said a word in spite of what they did. He looked across and caught my eye and, Dad, it was like he was suffering for me and you and Nan. Part of me wanted to stay with him – but I couldn't bear to see him suffer any more. I wonder how long he lasted.

PRAYER

Leader	Lord Jesus, you were the victim of cruel words.
	Help us to use our words to encourage, not to destroy.
All	Lord of the cross hear our prayer.

STATION 11 – JESUS IS NAILED TO THE CROSS

REUBEN

THE EXECUTIONER'S STORY

Hello! I'm home! What a day!

We had another three today. Two of them were straightforward. But I had to do another nail job. I really hate that. People think because it's my job I get used to doing it and I suppose I do to some extent. But I'll never get used to driving those six-inch nails into a man's wrists. The noise of the hammer on the nail and the hiss and crack as it enters the wrist make me sick. And then the poor soul's screaming, spitting and shouting and calling me all the names under the sun.

But this one today was a bit different. I recognised him, just. It was that young preacher from up north in Galilee – the one we saw in the Temple earlier in the week. I couldn't believe it. He seemed harmless enough – a bit of a dreamer really. I can't see what harm he'd have done anyone. Anyway, when I grabbed his arm, he didn't struggle, or swear or fight. I hit the nails in and the blood splattered all over my face and shirt and do you know what he said? He said, 'Father, forgive them'.

Now I don't know who he was talking to. Maybe he was delirious but it reminded me of when he said we had to forgive others as we would like to be forgiven. It was sort of proof that he really believed that forgiveness, not revenge, was the answer to Israel's problems. Tomorrow, I'm going to look for another job – because he's right.

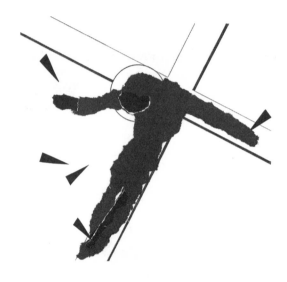

I don't know how many men I've executed – hundreds probably, maybe thousands – but I won't forget him. Yeshua from Nazareth – I won't forget him.

PRAYER

Leader   Lord Jesus,
you prayed for those
who murdered you.

Help us to pray for those who hurt us
that they may be changed
by the power of forgiveness.

All   Lord of the Cross
hear our prayer.

STATION 12 – JESUS DIES ON THE CROSS

LUCIUS
THE CENTURION'S STORY

Hello! I'm home! What a day!

We managed to knock off a bit early today, because of this Jewish Sabbath business. Apparently their day of rest starts at sunset, so all the crucifixions had to be over by then.

There was a big crowd today. It seems one of them was some sort of rebel leader. Anyway, Pilate doesn't like that sort of nonsense so we well and truly nailed him up.

We got the rebel and the other two up by nine o'clock and round about twelve the wind started to get up and the sky turned dark – so dark the sun was completely blacked out. It stayed like that and at about three, this rebel fellow started shrieking at the top of his voice, 'My God, my God, why have you deserted me?' It was sort of a song. And with that he looked up to the sky and the life sort of drained out of him.

Strange that he shouted out like that – like a wounded lion. He'd hardly said

anything up till then. But that scream – it went right through me and made the hairs on the back of my neck stand up. It's really got inside my head – it won't go away. I don't think I'll ever forget it.

But he was special all right, that fellow. The notice over his head said, 'Yeshua of Nazareth – King of the Jews'. And, do you know, he had more dignity than any of our emperors who call themselves gods. Yes, in a strange way this fellow was more like a god than any of them.

PRAYER

Leader   Lord Jesus,
the centurion recognised you as Son of God
in the moment of your death.

Help us to recognise you as the Son of God
who died to show each of us the power of love.

All   Lord of the Cross
hear our prayer.

32

STATION 13 – JESUS' BODY IS TAKEN FROM THE CROSS

JOSEPH OF ARIMATHAEA
THE COUNCILLOR'S STORY

Hello! I'm home! What a day!

And what a night! It all started for Nicodemus and me last night at Caiaphas' house. Caiaphas was interrogating that Galilean, Yeshua. I felt ashamed, you know, because the witnesses they called were lying about him and twisting his words, and I didn't say anything. Caiaphas is a powerful enemy to make and I just kept my mouth shut.

From there we went to Pilate's court, and he just washed his hands of it all and sent Yeshua off to be whipped and then crucified. I followed him all the way – it was terrible. Every step made me feel more and more guilty. And when they hoisted the cross up, it slipped into its block hole – and his body jerked and his shoulders cracked as they dislocated. And I stood there and watched him die. Transfixed like a young deer about to be consumed by a lion. I couldn't move. The sky went black and eventually he died.

At last, I had the courage to do something and I went to Pilate to ask to take his body. I was shaking, and God knows what Caiaphas will say when he finds out. Anyway, Pilate said yes. I don't think he was bothered at all. When I got back to Golgotha, and told the soldiers,

they said they'd have to check if he was really dead and not faking it. So they jabbed a spear into his side and out came a trickle of blood mixed with water. He was dead – and they knew it.

One of the executioners climbed up a ladder they put next to the cross and managed to get the nails out and they let his limp body fall to the floor. One of the executioners saw his mother was there and had the decency to lift his body into her arms. What a sight! Then, Nicodemus and I wrapped him in a cloth and picked him up and carried him to the tomb I bought for us. We put him in the tomb, and got some other chaps to help us roll a stone across the entrance. At last, I felt I'd done something for him. I just wish I'd done something earlier – then maybe none of this would have happened.

PRAYER

Leader   Lord Jesus,
            your mother cried for you
            and cradled you in birth and in death.

            Help us to cry with those who suffer
            and look after them in their sorrow.

All   Lord of the Cross
            hear our prayer.

STATION 14 – JESUS IS LAID IN THE TOMB

MARY

THE MOTHER OF JAMES' STORY

Hello! I'm home! What a day!

I can't believe what's happened. He's gone – dead! Yeshua's dead!

They nailed him to a cross and all he'd ever taught was to love one another. Why was he such a danger to the chief priests and Romans? And where were you? I thought you were his friend!

While you and the rest were hiding, I stayed till it was all over. Six hours he hung there. Then the centurion wouldn't release his body to us. It wasn't until Joseph of Arimathaea and Nicodemus came that they took him down. I don't know why they wanted him. They were part of the Sanhedrin that condemned him. If they wanted to help, why didn't they speak up for him when he was being questioned? The cowards!

Anyway, they took his body and Mary Magdalene and I followed them. We wanted to know where they were taking him and, would you believe it, they put him in this big tomb – the sort only the rich can afford! I can imagine what Yeshua would have said. He'd have said, 'Bury me with the poor – that's where I belong.'

So, they put him in the tomb and rolled a big stone across the opening without even washing his body and putting oil on it. I'll bet it was because the Sabbath was about to begin. But, I ask you, which is more important – a religious law or doing what's right for another person?

I know what Yeshua would say about that, too!

PRAYER

Leader Lord Jesus,
because of a religious law
you were buried without ceremony
in the tomb of a stranger.

Help us not to hide behind rules and regulations
and use them as excuses for not caring for others.

All Lord of the Cross
hear our prayer.

STATION 15 – JESUS RISES FROM THE DEAD

PETER

THE DISCIPLE'S STORY

Hello! I'm home! What a day!

I can't believe it, but it's happened. Yeshua's alive! He's risen from the dead! Oh, some people have said we've stolen his body – but it's not true – he must be alive!

It all started when Mary and Salome came here first thing – well, you were here then. They were hysterical, but we had to see for ourselves. John and I ran back to the graveyard and they were right. The stone had been rolled back. There was no way they could have done it. Outside were the cloths they'd wrapped him in – just lying on the ground. I went in, not knowing what I'd find, and there was the cloth they covered his face with – neatly rolled up.

We didn't know what to do, so we started walking home and then Mary Magdalene ran over to us and said she'd seen him – Yeshua! She thought he was the gardener at first, because he looked different in some way. But then she recognised him. I don't know what to believe. It just can't be true, yet I've got

this feeling. And I remember him saying that he was going to suffer and rise again. He kept going on about it – and I didn't understand. But he kept saying it. And he's been right about everything else. He said I'd deny him. How did he know? He said the chief priests were out to get him even before he got to Jerusalem – and they were.

Maybe he's right about this too. It sounds insane, but . . . oh my God! . . . look . . . Yeshua! . . . My Lord and my God!

PRAYER

Leader   Lord Jesus,
even when you rose from the dead
some of your friends doubted.

Help us to have the faith to recognise you
as Our Lord and Our God.

All   Lord of the Cross
hear our prayer.